D1011793

THIS BOOK BELONGS TO

_____

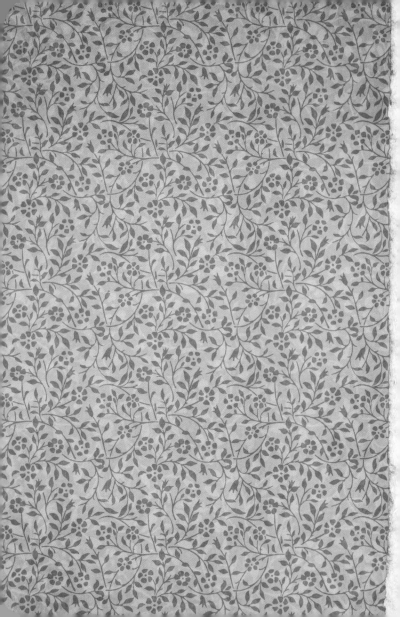

PRAYERS & PROMISES
FOR
Depression
and
Anxiety

BroadStreet
PUBLISHING

CONTENTS

Introduction

When life's troubles overwhelm you and you feel yourself slipping into depression or filled with anxiety, find your peace in God. Take comfort in knowing that he cares deeply for you and he will be with you in your darkest moments.

Prayers & Promises for Depression and Anxiety is a topically organized collection that guides you through themes of compassion, confidence, courage, identity, inspiration, purpose, and more. Encouraging Scriptures, heartfelt prayers, and prompting questions give you an opportunity to think more deeply about the hope found in God's Word.

Begin to experience underlying joy and peace as you dwell on the promises of God.

Abandonment

"The LORD himself goes before you and will be with you;
he will never leave you nor forsake you."

DEUTERONOMY 31:8 NIV

The LORD loves justice and fairness;
he will never abandon his people.
They will be kept safe forever.

PSALM 37:28 TLB

God makes a home for the lonely;
He leads out the prisoners into prosperity.

PSALM 68:6 NASB

"I will not abandon you as orphans—
I will come to you."

JOHN 14:18 NLT

God, you say over and over in your Word that you will not leave me. Give me eyes to see you when I feel alone. Let my heart know your nearness when I cry out to you. You never turn away from those who need you, and oh, how I need you!

I will cling to the truth that your ever-present help is at hand, especially when I've reached the end of my rope. Today, may the comfort of your presence melt away every fear and lead me into love.

Do you truly believe that
God will never leave you?

Acceptance

"The Father gives me the people who are mine.
Every one of them will come to me,
and I will always accept them."

JOHN 6:37 NCV

The LORD does not see as man sees;
for man looks at the outward appearance,
but the LORD looks at the heart.

1 SAMUEL 16:7 NKJV

If God is for us, who can be against us?

ROMANS 8:31 ESV

Before he made the world, God chose us to be his very
own through what Christ would do for us; he decided
then to make us holy in his eyes, without a single fault—
we who stand before him covered with his love.

EPHESIANS 1:4 TLB

God, what a wonder that you see me in a way that no one else does. Not only did you choose me before the beginning of time as your own, but nothing can change your mind about me! Thank you for accepting me just as I am, not as how I should be.

Help me to accept myself as you do and to know that I don't have to do anything to earn your love. As I learn to receive your love without condition, I pray that I will love the way you do.

How does God's acceptance of you help you be more accepting of others?

Adoption

You did not receive a spirit of slavery to fall back into fear, but you have received a spirit of adoption. When we cry, "Abba! Father!" it is that very Spirit bearing witness with our spirit that we are children of God.

ROMANS 8:15–16 NRSV

"I will bring the blind by a way they did not know;
I will lead them in paths they have not known.
I will make darkness light before them,
And crooked places straight.
These things will I do for them,
And not forsake them."

ISAIAH 42:16 NKJV

The LORD will not abandon His people on account of His great name, because the LORD has been pleased to make you a people for Himself.

1 SAMUEL 12:22 NASB

Father, how amazing it is that you call me your child! You do not leave your children to be tormented by their fears, so when I am afraid, I will run to you. You are my safe place, a refuge and help in time of trouble. I never need to hesitate to come to you, my good Father.

Thank you for welcoming me into your family; it is better than anything I've known. Help me to remember today, and every day, what my rights and privileges are as your child.

How does knowing that
God has adopted you into his family
make you feel?

Anxiety

You will keep in perfect peace
those whose minds are steadfast,
because they trust in you.

ISAIAH 26:3 NIV

"Don't let your hearts be troubled.
Trust in God, and trust also in me."

JOHN 14:1 NLT

Give all your worries to him,
because he cares about you.

1 PETER 5:7 NCV

I call out to the LORD when I'm in trouble,
and he answers me.

PSALM 120:1 NIRV

Lord, you know my heart and my every thought. You know when I sit and when I stand. You know my history and my future. There are no mysteries to you. When doubts and fears threaten to overwhelm my mind and body, be the peace that calms the storm.

I will remember who you are: Defender, Savior, the Good Shepherd. You are my hope. I will trust in you, even when it takes everything inside of me to choose it. I will remember that though I cannot see the way out, you see it all so clearly and you are never overwhelmed. I trust you, God.

What steps can you take to be less anxious and more trusting?

Assurance

To him who is able to do immeasurably more than all we ask or imagine, according to his power that is at work within us, to him be glory...for ever and ever! Amen.

EPHESIANS 3:20–21 NIV

All of God's promises have been fulfilled in Christ with a resounding "Yes!"

2 CORINTHIANS 1:20 NLT

Jesus Christ is the same yesterday and today and forever.

HEBREWS 13:8 NASB

These things I have written to you who believe in the name of the Son of God, that you may know that you have eternal life, and that you may continue to believe in the name of the Son of God.

1 JOHN 5:13 NKJV

God, I believe that you are who you say you are. Jesus, in you is the fulfillment of God's promise for salvation. Thank you for being faithful to your Word. In you I place my hope. I ask that you would do more than I can even think to imagine or ask for with my little life.

Help me to believe that you will come through even when it's hard for me to see a silver lining. You are better than my best day and more faithful than the rising sun.

How does believing God's promises cause you to feel reassured?

Beauty

You are altogether beautiful, my darling,
beautiful in every way.

Song of Songs 4:7 NLT

No, your beauty should come from within you—
the beauty of a gentle and quiet spirit that will
never be destroyed and is very precious to God.

1 Peter 3:4 NCV

She puts on strength and honor
as if they were her clothes.

Proverbs 31:25 NIRV

I praise you because you made me
in an amazing and wonderful way.
What you have done is wonderful.
I know this very well.

Psalm 139:14 NCV

Lord, when I look at the abundance of diversity in the world around me, I remember that beauty comes in many forms. When you created me, you did it intentionally.

Thank you that you made me unique on purpose and that beauty is so much more than skin-deep. Let beauty first grow in my heart, spilling out into the rest of my being. I praise you for I am fearfully and wonderfully made.

How does it make you feel to think God sees you as beautiful?

Belief

He must have a strong belief in the trustworthy message
he was taught; then he will be able to encourage others
with wholesome teaching and show those who oppose it
where they are wrong.

TITUS 1:9 NLT

If you instruct the brethren in these things,
you will be a good minister of Jesus Christ,
nourished in the words of faith and of the good
doctrine which you have carefully followed.

1 TIMOTHY 4:6 NKJV

"All things are possible to him who believes."

MARK 9:23 NASB

"Have you believed because you have seen me? Blessed
are those who have not seen and yet have believed."

JOHN 20:29 ESV

Jesus, I believe that you are the Son of God. You came to earth as a human so that we could know what the Father is really like. Above all, you taught us what it means to love without condition. I believe who you were, you still are, and I can trust you with my life.

Thank you for the gift of knowing you. I pray that my belief would lead me into greater confidence in my relationship with you. Thank you that you are near and not distant. Whatever happens in the world around me, I believe that you remain constant.

How can you strengthen your belief in God?

Blessings

Surely, LORD, you bless those who do what is right.
Like a shield, your loving care keeps them safe.

PSALM 5:12 NIRV

Surely you have granted him unending blessings
and made him glad with the joy of your presence.

PSALM 21:6 NIV

Give praise to the God and Father of our Lord Jesus
Christ. He has blessed us with every spiritual blessing.
Those blessings come from the heavenly world. They
belong to us because we belong to Christ. God chose us to
belong to Christ before the world was created. He chose
us to be holy and without blame in his eyes. He loved us.

EPHESIANS 1:3-4 NIRV

Lord, when I take time to recognize what I have to be thankful for, I realize that your goodness is all around me. When I am feeling overwhelmed, I can practice counting my blessings. The biggest blessing I have is your presence.

May the joy of your presence awaken me to life and to your goodness in and around me. I know that you are the giver of all good gifts; today I will be on the lookout for them, knowing that nothing is too big or too small for you.

Which of God's blessings come to your mind today?

Boldness

He proclaimed the kingdom of God
and taught about the Lord Jesus Christ—
with all boldness and without hindrance!

ACTS 28:31 NIV

Sinners run away even when no one is chasing them.
But those who do what is right are as bold as lions.

PROVERBS 28:1 NIRV

On the day I called you, you answered me.
You made me strong and brave.

PSALM 138:3 NCV

Let us come boldly to the throne of our gracious God.
There we will receive his mercy, and we will find grace to
help us when we need it most.

HEBREWS 4:16 NLT

Lord, if I have any strength, I know it comes from you. Let me walk boldly into the situations I face, confident that you are with me. With you, there is no need to be timid. I can be courageous in life because I know I can be bold with you. It is in your presence that I am met with the mercy and tenderness of a good father. It is where I receive everything I need.

When I am feeling frozen, stuck, or timid, would you remind me of who you are and who I am in you? You have always been faithful to call me into my best self. I want to be like you, both bold and tender-hearted. Help me to remember that courage does not require perfection, only willingness.

Why is it sometimes hard to be bold?

Change

Look! I tell you this secret:
We will not all sleep in death,
but we will all be changed.

1 CORINTHIANS 15:51 NCV

He will take our weak mortal bodies and change them
into glorious bodies like his own, using the same power
with which he will bring everything under his control.

PHILIPPIANS 3:21 NLT

Jesus Christ is the same yesterday and today and forever.

HEBREWS 13:8 NIRV

Lord, when change threatens to overwhelm me, help me to remember that change brings with it hope for better things ahead. When it feels as if the bottom has dropped out of life and I don't know what my future will look like, I know that I can trust in you. You stay the same forever, and there are no mysteries to you.

You see and know every step of my journey. You know the end from the beginning and you are not surprised by anything. I trust in you, the unchanging one.

How do you handle change?

Compassion

When I am with those who are weak,
I share their weakness,
for I want to bring the weak to Christ.
Yes, I try to find common ground with everyone,
doing everything I can to save some.

1 Corinthians 9:22 NLT

God, have mercy on me according to your faithful love.
Because your love is so tender and kind,
wipe out my lawless acts.

Psalm 51:1 NIRV

Praise be to the God and Father of our Lord Jesus Christ,
the Father of compassion and the God of all comfort.

2 Corinthians 1:3 NIV

Father of compassion, you are the source of all comfort. You are so kind and patient toward me. Even when I have what feels like nothing to offer, you so willingly draw near with your unfailing love. In my weakness, you don't turn away from me.

In the same way, help me not to run away from weakness I see in others; I want to be like you, lavishly loving those who have nothing to offer me. Thank you for loving better than anyone I've ever known or can imagine.

How can you be a more compassionate person?

Comfort

May our Lord Jesus Christ himself and God our Father,
who loved us and by his grace gave us eternal comfort
and a wonderful hope, comfort you and strengthen you.

2 THESSALONIANS 2:16–17 NLT

Unless the LORD had helped me,
I would soon have settled in the silence of the grave.
I cried out, "I am slipping!"
but your unfailing love, O LORD, supported me.
When doubts filled my mind,
your comfort gave me renewed hope and cheer.

PSALM 94:17–19 NLT

To all who mourn… he will give: beauty for ashes;
joy instead of mourning; praise instead of heaviness.
For God has planted them like strong and
graceful oaks for his own glory.

ISAIAH 61:3 TLB

God, my God, I cannot face my sadness without you. I would be swept away without the light of your love beckoning me to shore. When I am in the throes of grief and sorrow, you are the only peace I know. Help. When I can only mutter that word, rush in with the comfort of your presence, covering me in your overwhelming love.

Let the peace that passes understanding spread through me like the warmth of the sun. When I grieve, I know that you are with me; though it may be an end, it is not the end. Breathe hope into my life again when I need it the most.

Do you feel the comforting presence of God today?

Confidence

I can do everything through Christ,
who gives me strength.

PHILIPPIANS 4:13 NLT

Be my rock of refuge,
to which I can always go;
give the command to save me,
for you are my rock and my fortress....
For you have been my hope, Sovereign LORD,
my confidence since my youth.

PSALM 71:3, 5 NIV

Do not throw away your confidence,
which has a great reward.

HEBREWS 10:35 NCV

Lord, when I have nothing to stand on except your Word, be my strength. When I don't know what to do or where to turn, I turn to you. You have not failed me yet, and I believe that you will be faithfully with me every step of my journey.

Thank you that my confidence is not meant to be found in myself—what a relief! I come to you again today. Be my rock of refuge and my fortress, my safe place where I find rest from the storms of life.

How do you find your confidence?

Contentment

To enjoy your work and to accept your lot in life—that is
indeed a gift from God. The person who does that will
not need to look back with sorrow on his past, for God
gives him joy.

ECCLESIASTES 5:20 TLB

I know what it is to be in need, and I know what it is to
have plenty. I have learned the secret of being content
in any and every situation, whether well fed or hungry,
whether living in plenty or in want. I can do all this
through him who gives me strength.

PHILIPPIANS 4:12-13 NIV

Lord, help me to look at my life and see the gifts within it. Give me eyes to see the beauty of the people you have surrounded me with and the honor it is to serve and love them. Your Word makes it clear that contentment has less to do with what I have and more to do with how I see it.

May my mind be trained to see with the lens of plenty, not through the aperture of lack. As I practice the gratitude of what is, rather than what could be, may your joy fill me like a fountain!

How can you choose to be content with your life as it is right now?

Courage

Be strong in the Lord and in his mighty power.
Put on the full armor of God, so that you can take your
stand against the devil's schemes.

EPHESIANS 6:10-11 NIV

Be alert. Continue strong in the faith.
Have courage, and be strong. Do everything in love.

1 CORINTHIANS 16:13-14 NCV

Even though I walk through the darkest valley,
I will not be afraid. You are with me.
Your shepherd's rod and staff comfort me.

PSALM 23:4 NIRV

"This is my command—be strong and courageous!
Do not be afraid or discouraged.
For the LORD your God is with you wherever you go."

JOSHUA 1:9 NLT

God, thank you that you are with me wherever I am! I know that I can face anything with you as my constant companion. When I walk through darkness and I cannot see the light of day, I trust that you will guide me through the night with your steady hand. You never falter, and neither will your grip on me.

When I am afraid, I will trust in you and find my strength in your love. I will not give up even when it is hard to remember what I'm fighting for. Sweep in and remind me that you have been faithful at every turn and will continue to be.

When was the last time you asked God for courage?

Delight

When I received your words, I ate them.
They filled me with joy. My heart took delight in them.
LORD God who rules over all, I belong to you.

JEREMIAH 15:16 NIRV

"My God, I want to do what you want.
Your teachings are in my heart."

PSALM 40:8 NCV

Your laws are my treasure;
they are my heart's delight.

PSALM 119:111 NLT

"Let your light shine before others, that they may see
your good deeds and glorify your Father in heaven."

MATTHEW 5:16 NIV

God, giver of all joy, I sometimes forget how happy you are. Father, you say that you delight in your children—you delight in me! What a mind-blowing reality. Let your revelation shine in my mind like the rising sun, bringing light to areas that have been hidden in darkness.

Your joy over me being yours fills my heart with incredible wonder. How could I do anything but be delighted by you? Thank you for your love that surprises me in the best of ways. You are amazing in your unwavering opinion of me.

How hard is it for you to fathom God's incredible delight in you?

Deliverance

Humble yourselves in the sight of the Lord,
and He will lift you up.

JAMES 4:10 NKJV

My prayer is to you, O LORD.
At an acceptable time, O God,
in the abundance of your steadfast love
answer me in your saving faithfulness.
Deliver me from sinking in the mire;
let me be delivered from my enemies
and from the deep waters.
Answer me, O LORD, for your steadfast love is good;
according to your abundant mercy, turn to me.

PSALM 69:13-14, 16 ESV

The righteous person faces many troubles,
but the LORD comes to the rescue each time.

PSALM 34:19 NLT

Lord, you alone know the extent of the troubles I face. You know when I'm tired, defeated, and feel like giving up. Rush in with your faithful love and save me. Deliver me from the fear that threatens my peace; be my defender and my advocate. I cannot save myself, and when I start sinking, I don't even want to.

You, God, are stronger than my fiercest enemies. Your goodness speaks louder than the lies; I can hear the echoes of your goodness, and I trust that you will help me every time I need it. Lift me up, God, you're all I have.

Can you ask God for deliverance from your fears?

Depression

The LORD hears his people when they call to him for help.
He rescues them from all their troubles.

PSALM 34:17 NLT

Why am I so sad? Why am I so upset?
I should put my hope in God
and keep praising him.

PSALM 42:11 NCV

You, O LORD, are a shield about me, my glory,
and the lifter of my head.

PSALM 3:3 ESV

He has delivered us from the power of darkness and
conveyed us into the kingdom of the Son of His love.

COLOSSIANS 1:13 NKJV

Faithful Father, I need you to be the lifter of my head. When darkness clouds my mind and settles over me like an unwelcome haze, I know I cannot wish it away. You, God, are my deliverer. I will choose to put my hope in you no matter what I'm feeling.

Please do the heavy lifting here, Lord. As I choose you, do what only you can do. Let the light of your love shine through the fog of despair and loneliness, bringing relief and freedom. You are my only hope.

Can you sense God's comfort and
joy in the middle of your sadness?

Encouragement

The LORD your God is with you;
the mighty One will save you.
He will rejoice over you. You will rest in his love;
he will sing and be joyful about you.

ZEPHANIAH 3:17 NCV

Nothing is more appealing than speaking
beautiful, life-giving words.
For they release sweetness to our souls
and inner healing to our spirits.

PROVERBS 16:24 TPT

Be joyful. Grow to maturity. Encourage each other.
Live in harmony and peace. Then the God of love and
peace will be with you.

2 CORINTHIANS 13:11 NLT

Lord, thank you that I was made for relationship. First, would you speak your words over me, bringing life to my whole being? God of love and peace, may my words be filled with kindness, dripping with grace. I believe that even when I am feeling down, when I encourage others, I will be encouraged myself.

Let me be someone who calls out the treasure I see in those around me. As you do the same with me, my heart will be strengthened, and my soul will breathe deeply of your love.

How can you encourage someone today?

Eternity

We are citizens of heaven, where the Lord Jesus Christ
lives. And we are eagerly waiting for him to return
as our Savior.

PHILIPPIANS 3:20 NLT

That will happen in a flash, as quickly as you can wink an
eye. It will happen at the blast of the last trumpet. Then the
dead will be raised to live forever. And we will be changed.

1 CORINTHIANS 15:52 NIRV

Why would I fear the future?
For your goodness and love pursue me
all the days of my life.
Then afterward, when my life is through,
I'll return to your glorious presence
to be forever with you!

PSALM 23:6 TPT

Lord, I thank you that this life isn't all there is. When I have hard days, help me to remember that the taste of your goodness and love I experience here on earth are glimpses of a greater reality. When I dwell in eternity with you, there will be no more sin. There will be no more fear, and there will be no more injustice.

Thank you that what I have to look forward to is greater than anything I've known. Remind me that the best is yet to come when I start to forget. I will trust you!

Can you view eternity with a hopeful, happy heart, fully trusting in a good God?

Faith

Through Christ you have come to trust in God. And you
have placed your faith and hope in God because he raised
Christ from the dead and gave him great glory.

1 PETER 1:21 NLT

"What I'm about to tell you is true. If you have faith as
small as a mustard seed, it is enough. You can say to this
mountain, 'Move from here to there.' And it will move.
Nothing will be impossible for you."

MATTHEW 17:20 NIRV

The important thing is faith—
the kind of faith that works through love.

GALATIANS 5:6 NCV

Faith is confidence in what we hope for
and assurance about what we do not see.

HEBREWS 11:1 NIV

Father, when my faith is as small as a mustard seed, let me be reminded that it is enough to move a mountain. Today, with the size of faith I have, I tell the mountains of depression and anxiety to be moved!

May your light shine on me and bring relief. Where there has been confusion and the feeling of being stuck, let the ground be leveled so I can see the path before me. Whatever it looks like, I know one thing—it leads me to you.

What gives you faith and hope in Jesus?

Faithfulness

Your lovingkindness, O Lord, extends to the heavens,
Your faithfulness reaches to the skies.

PSALM 36:5 NASB

The Lord is faithful, who will establish you
and guard you from the evil one.

2 THESSALONIANS 3:3 NKJV

Lord, you are my God; I will exalt you and praise
your name, for in perfect faithfulness you have done
wonderful things, things planned long ago.

ISAIAH 25:1 NIV

The word of the Lord is upright,
and all his work is done in faithfulness.

PSALM 33:4 ESV

Faithful Father, I cannot forget how you have been with me. When I start to question whether you are here now, I look back on my history with you and I see it—I see your faithfulness. You don't change your mind about things or people, and you haven't changed your mind about wanting me as your own.

As your child, I cling to you in my weakness. I trust you to do what only you can do. Finish the work you have started and make my paths straight.

How have you seen the faithfulness of God played out in your life?

Fear

God gave us his Spirit. And the Spirit doesn't make us
weak and fearful. Instead, the Spirit gives us power and
love. He helps us control ourselves.

2 TIMOTHY 1:7 NIRV

The LORD is my light and my salvation—
whom shall I fear?
The LORD is the stronghold of my life—
of whom shall I be afraid?

PSALM 27:1 NIV

When I am afraid, I will trust you.
I praise God for his word.
I trust God, so I am not afraid.
What can human beings do to me?

PSALM 56:3-4 NCV

Lord of my life, you are my helper. You are my safe place and my salvation. I come to you with my fear, knowing that in your presence, you bring peace and rest. Your Spirit gives me power when I feel helpless. Thank you that I never need to stay in a place of worry or despair.

When I come to you, let me hear your perfect truth about my life and your good intentions for me. Fear cannot remain when your perfect love comes in. Thank you for the power of your love.

What fears can you give to God right now?

Freedom

Where the Spirit of the Lord is, there is freedom.

2 Corinthians 3:17 niv

Beloved ones, God has called us to live a life of freedom
in the Holy Spirit. But don't view this wonderful freedom
as an opportunity to set up a base of operations in the
natural realm. Freedom means that we become so
completely free of self-indulgence that we become
servants of one another, expressing love in all we do.

Galatians 5:13 tpt

"So if the Son sets you free, you are truly free."

John 8:36 nlt

We have freedom now, because Christ made us free.
So stand strong. Do not change and go back into the
slavery of the law.

Galatians 5:1 ncv

Jesus, I know that you came to set the captives free. That means whatever areas I am feeling bound by—sin, fear, or sickness—you have already overcome. When I am feeling stuck, I remember that you chose me to be free. Overwhelm my circumstances with the power of your resurrection, setting me free from any chains.

Your ways are so much better than my own, and you move in purpose and power. I invite you into my day; come and set my feet free to dance upon worry, disappointment, and despair. You are greater!

How does it feel to be free from your sin?

Friendship

A friend loves you all the time,
and a brother helps in time of trouble.

PROVERBS 17:17 NCV

There are "friends" who destroy each other,
but a real friend sticks closer than a brother.

PROVERBS 18:24 NLT

"Greater love has no one than this: to lay down one's
life for one's friends. You are my friends if you do what
I command.... Instead, I have called you friends, for
everything that I learned from my Father I have made
known to you."

JOHN 15:13-15 NIV

"In everything, do to others what you would want them to
do to you."

MATTHEW 7:12 NIRV

Jesus, you are my closest friend. No one knows me the way you do. And yet, you have surrounded me with people who know and love me. Help me, when I am feeling isolated and alone, to reach out to you and to the people I love and trust.

I also want to be a friend that lays down my own preferences for the good of those I love. Thank you that you created us to be in relationship, not to live alone. Today, as I connect with others around me, may it draw me closer to you.

What friends spur you on in your relationship with God?

Goodness

Everything God created is good, and nothing is to be
rejected if it is received with thanksgiving.

1 TIMOTHY 4:4 NIV

Taste and see that the LORD is good.
Oh, the joys of those who take refuge in him!

PSALM 34:8 NLT

My brothers and sisters, I am sure that you are full of
goodness. I know that you have all the knowledge you
need and that you are able to teach each other.

ROMANS 15:14 NCV

Lord, your goodness knows no end. Even when it feels like chaos threatens to drown out the truth of this, I will force myself to remember that all good things come from you. Help me to seek out the goodness in my life—nothing is too small to celebrate.

I look for your goodness like a child looking for treasure in the world around them. Thank you that when I look for it, I will find it.

Where do you see the goodness of God the most in your life?

Grace

From his fullness we have all received, grace upon grace.

John 1:16 NRSV

God gives us even more grace, as the Scripture says,
"God is against the proud, but he gives grace to the
humble."

James 4:6 NCV

Remember this: sin will not conquer you,
for God already has!
You are not governed by law
but governed by the reign of the grace of God.

Romans 6:14 TPT

God, your grace speaks of your kindness. You offer it in abundance to all, especially to those needing it the most. Thank you that your unmerited favor is freely given, and I don't have to prove that I deserve it.

Today I remember that your grace has nothing to do with whether or not I do enough. I'm so thankful that it has nothing to do with me. I receive your grace in this moment, knowing that it is never like stale bread. You give what is good and right and needed at the right time, and even more than I can ask.

What does God's grace look like in your life?

Grief

Those who sow in tears shall reap with shouts of joy.

PSALM 126:5 ESV

Let your steadfast love become my comfort
according to your promise to your servant.

PSALM 119:76 NRSV

"Come to me, all you who are weary and burdened, and I
will give you rest. Take my yoke upon you and learn from
me, for I am gentle and humble in heart, and you will
find rest for your souls."

MATTHEW 11:28-29 NIV

Every valley shall be raised up,
every mountain and hill made low;
the rough ground shall become level,
the rugged places a plain.

ISAIAH 40:4 NIV

All-knowing One, I come to you with the burdens weighing
me down. Grief has ripped my heart to shreds. You say that
you give rest. Oh, how I need that right now! When I am
overcome by sadness at the loss of what could have been,
surround me with your comfort and your presence of peace.

When I can't even reach out to you, lift me up. You're all I have
and the only one who truly knows the depths of what I'm
walking through. Let your love surround me and bring hope.

Do you ask God for help
when you need his comfort?

Guidance

Guide me in your truth and teach me,
for you are God my Savior,
and my hope is in you all day long.

PSALM 25:5 NIV

Wise people can also listen and learn;
even they can find good advice in these words.

PROVERBS 1:5 NCV

We can make our plans,
but the LORD determines our steps.

PROVERBS 16:9 NLT

Those who are led by the Spirit of God
are children of God.

ROMANS 8:14 NIRV

Good Father, I trust that you are leading my steps. You know how much I depend on your guidance. All my hopes are in you. Even when my plans crumble and there is a detour in my path, I trust that you have better plans than I do.

You see the full picture; there are no mysteries to you. I trust that your ways are higher than my ways, and your plans are better than the ones I pursue for myself. I yield to your leadership in my life and shrug off the worries of the unknown. You are a good and faithful leader.

Is there anything God can help guide you in today?

Guilt

God is faithful and fair. If we confess our sins, he will
forgive our sins. He will forgive every wrong thing we
have done. He will make us pure.

1 John 1:9 NIRV

The Lord and King helps me. He won't let me be
dishonored. So I've made up my mind to keep on serving
him. I know he won't let me be put to shame.

Isaiah 50:7 NIRV

Those who go to him for help are happy,
and they are never disgraced.

Psalm 34:5 NCV

I have not achieved it, but I focus on this one thing:
Forgetting the past and looking forward to what
lies ahead.

Philippians 3:13 NLT

Loving God, forgiver of my sins, may the purpose of guilt be that it leads me to reconciliation with you and with others. I don't want to be stuck in a cycle of guilt and shame that does nothing but punish me. You are the one who set me free, so I will be free! You have made me clean already.

I am not too proud to say when I have messed up. Thank you that I don't need to live in the torment of "could haves" and "should haves." I look to you, the author and finisher of my faith, to lead me into the fullness of forgiveness.

Why doesn't God want you to feel guilt and shame?

Health

The world and its desires pass away,
but whoever does the will of God lives forever.

1 JOHN 2:17 NIV

Don't think for a moment that you know it all, for
wisdom comes when you adore him with undivided
devotion and avoid everything that's wrong.
Then you will find the healing refreshment your body
and spirit long for.

PROVERBS 3:7-8 TPT

I will never forget your commandments,
for by them you give me life.

PSALM 119:93 NLT

A happy heart is like good medicine,
but a broken spirit drains your strength.

PROVERBS 17:22 NCV

Lord, I know that you care about every part of my life. You are not just concerned with my soul, but you also care about every part of my being. My mind and body are as important to you as my heart. Lord, I trust that you are my healer. Would you touch me today with your healing power, driving every sickness out, healing every broken part?

Thank you for knowing me inside out. I pray that your kingdom would come on earth as it is in heaven—in my body. I am desperate for your help.

What healing are you believing God for right now?

Hope

The LORD is good to those whose hope is in him,
to the one who seeks him.

LAMENTATIONS 3:25 NIV

Hope will never bring us shame. That's because God's
love has poured into our hearts. This happened through
the Holy Spirit, who has been given to us.

ROMANS 5:5 NIRV

The LORD's delight is in those who fear him,
those who put their hope in his unfailing love.

PSALM 147:11 NLT

God my hope, you are the one I look to today. Meet me in this moment, breathing life into my weary heart. Fill my mind with your peace. When my path gets bumpy and I am uncertain at how things will turn out, I turn to you.

I don't have to know how everything will play out in my life— I just need to know you. I need to know who you are. In you I find my hope. Come close, Lord, and lift my head. Your unfailing love surrounds me.

Knowing that God always hears you, what can you be hopeful for?

Identity

See how very much our Father loves us, for he calls us
his children, and that is what we are! But the people who
belong to this world don't recognize that we are God's
children because they don't know him. Dear friends,
we are already God's children, but he has not yet shown
us what we will be like when Christ appears. But we do
know that we will be like him, for we will see him
as he really is.

1 JOHN 3:1-2 NLT

Do everything without grumbling or arguing, so that
you may become blameless and pure, "children of God
without fault in a warped and crooked generation." Then
you will shine among them like stars in the sky as you
hold firmly to the word of life.

PHILIPPIANS 2:14-16 NIV

Loving God, thank you that you have called me your child. I get all the benefits of being your kid—that is almost unfathomable! Oh, how I want to be more like you. Thank you that you are changing me into your image even through the hard and dry seasons.

When I don't know anything else, I remember that you have called me child. You didn't call me an acquaintance, servant, or distant relative. Father, let my heart be rooted in this close relationship, knowing that you care for me. Shepherd me and teach me to be like you.

Who do you think God really sees when he looks at you?

Inspiration

The precepts of the LORD are right, giving joy to the heart.
The commands of the LORD are radiant,
giving light to the eyes.

PSALM 19:8 NIV

Your laws are my treasure;
they are my heart's delight.

PSALM 119:111 NLT

The whole Bible was given to us by inspiration from
God and is useful to teach us what is true and to make us
realize what is wrong in our lives; it straightens us out
and helps us do what is right.

2 TIMOTHY 3:16 TLB

God, you are the Creator of all things. Knowing that I was made in your image means I was also intended to create. When you lift my burdens and bring light to my eyes, there is nowhere that I can look that I won't find inspiration. Thank you that you are the source of all inspiring thoughts and ideas.

You bring revelation of your kingdom and your ways. You are my delight; I will not forget that! I will remember every good gift you have given, knowing that you are the greatest of them all. Give me eyes to see your creativity and intention in creation today.

How do you find inspiration?

Joy

May the God of hope fill you with all joy and peace as you
trust in him, so that you may overflow with hope by the
power of the Holy Spirit.

ROMANS 15:13 NIV

"Don't be sad, because the joy of the LORD
will make you strong."

NEHEMIAH 8:10 NCV

The LORD is my strength and shield.
I trust him with all my heart.
He helps me, and my heart is filled with joy.
I burst out in songs of thanksgiving.

PSALM 28:7 NLT

Always be joyful because you belong to the Lord.
I will say it again. Be joyful!

PHILIPPIANS 4:4 NIRV

God, you say that you give joy to your people. I need to know what it means for your joy to be my strength. Infuse my weary soul today with hope, peace, and relief. I have tasted your joy before, but it almost seems like a distant memory. Would you refresh my soul with the strength of your love?

Rescue me from the troubles that threaten to take me out. Then I will burst into songs of thanksgiving; I will shout for joy, knowing that you have not left me!

What is one truly joyful moment you've had recently?

Kindness

Be kind to each other, tenderhearted, forgiving one another, just as God through Christ has forgiven you.

EPHESIANS 4:32 NLT

Kind people do themselves a favor,
but cruel people bring trouble on themselves.

PROVERBS 11:17 NCV

Do you disrespect God's great kindness and favor?
Do you disrespect God when he is patient with you?
Don't you realize that God's kindness is meant to turn
you away from your sins?

ROMANS 2:4 NIRV

Great is his love toward us,
and the faithfulness of the LORD endures forever.
Praise the LORD.

PSALM 117:2 NIV

In your unfailing love, God, I see your kindness. You are so patient. Help me to also be kind in the waiting. Let me be one who forgives quickly, letting go of offense and resentment. I do not want to become a hardened shell of a person in these hard times.

Help my heart to stay tender, remembering how much I benefit from your kindness, so I will offer the same to others. Today, I yield my heart to you again, knowing the One who holds it is kind and good.

How can you extend kindness to those around you today?

Life

All praise to God, the Father of our Lord Jesus Christ.
It is by his great mercy that we have been born again,
because God raised Jesus Christ from the dead.
Now we live with great expectation.

1 PETER 1:3 NLT

That faith and that knowledge come from the hope for life
forever, which God promised to us before time began.

TITUS 1:2 NCV

"I am the way and the truth and the life.
No one comes to the Father except through me."

JOHN 14:6 NIRV

Jesus, you said that you are life. When it feels like I just want to give up and I question the point of these harsh times, I look to you. I have tasted and seen the goodness of walking in the land of the living, and I believe I will know it again! Help me not to give up when life goes differently than how I imagined it would. You know all things, and I can trust that you are not surprised.

Thank you, oh thank you, for the coming age where I will live forever with you and there will be no more sickness, sadness, injustice, or death. What a glorious reality to look forward to.

What is your favorite part of life?

Loneliness

"Teach them to obey everything that I have taught you, and
I will be with you always, even until the end of this age."

Matthew 28:20 ncv

The Lord is near to all who call on him,
yes, to all who call on him in truth.

Psalm 145:18 nlt

Even if my father and mother abandon me,
the Lord will hold me close.

Psalm 27:10 nlt

"Be strong and courageous. Do not be afraid or terrified
because of them, for the Lord your God goes with you;
he will never leave you nor forsake you."

Deuteronomy 31:6 niv

Lord my God, I need you to meet me right where I am, in the midst of my loneliness. You said that you will never leave or forsake me. I need to know the reality of that in the comfort of your presence. When I feel like no one understands what I am going through, or would even care to, you remind me that you never turn away. You are with me in my mess and my failure. You are with me in the mundane and the ordinary.

I will not stop calling on you. You are all I have. Come through again, Lord, with your peace and life. Let the closeness of our friendship be the foundation of my life and every other relationship.

When you feel lonely, can you turn to
God and ask him to surround you
with his presence?

Loss

Those who sow in tears shall reap with shouts of joy.

PSALM 126:5 ESV

Let your steadfast love become my comfort
according to your promise to your servant.

PSALM 119:76 NRSV

The earth may fall apart.
The mountains may fall into the middle of the sea.
But we will not be afraid.
The waters of the sea may roar and foam.
The mountains may shake when the waters rise.
But we will not be afraid.
God's blessings are like a river.
They fill the city of God with joy.

PSALM 46:2-4 NIRV

Faithful One, when loss seems to rip the ground out from beneath my feet, I will call out to you. I cannot articulate how deeply my heart hurts; I need to know your comfort and your nearness. I have so many questions, but I don't know that any answers would satisfy. As I grieve the loss before me, I will not sweep my feelings under the rug. I come to you, knowing that you understand even if that doesn't feel like enough right now.

When I cannot call out for help, you are there. Thank you for being compassionate, patient, and kind. And thank you that there is hope for the future. You never change. I see that you are my constant, faithful friend. You are with me in this.

Do you ask God for help when you need his comfort?

Love

Three things will last forever—faith, hope, and love—
and the greatest of these is love.

1 Corinthians 13:13 nlt

Lord, you are good. You are forgiving.
You are full of love for all who call out to you.

Psalm 86:5 nirv

Fill us with your love every morning.
Then we will sing and rejoice all our lives.

Psalm 90:14 ncv

Let love and faithfulness never leave you;
bind them around your neck,
write them on the tablet of your heart.

Proverbs 3:3 niv

God, your love is unlike any love I've ever known. I get to love you because you loved me first. Love is not just an idea; it is an expression of your very character. Fill me with your love today. Thank you that it is not conditional; you never withhold love from those who come to you.

Your love is radical, and I know that if anything can radically change my heart, it is that. Let your perfect love drive out every fear that threatens to keep me captive. May your love be the fuel that keeps me moving toward you and engaging with those around me. There is nothing that your love doesn't cover.

How does the love of God in your life help you to love others?

Patience

Warn those who are lazy.
Encourage those who are timid.
Take tender care of those who are weak.
Be patient with everyone.

1 Thessalonians 5:14 nlt

Be like those who through faith and patience
will receive what God has promised.

Hebrews 6:12 ncv

Be completely humble and gentle;
be patient, bearing with one another in love.

Ephesians 4:2 niv

Anyone who is patient has great understanding.
But anyone who gets angry quickly shows how foolish
they are.

Proverbs 14:29 nirv

God, you know that waiting is hard for me. I know that process is your protocol—most things don't come quickly or easily. I want to be a person who has incredible patience and grace for myself and for those around me. When the day at hand feels overwhelming and pointless, help me to see it as part of the bigger picture.

Help me to have a broader perspective to know that my decisions and attitudes in the moment have a ripple effect on those around me and on my future. I know that when you meet me in this aspect of my life my heart will change for the better.

How can you show more patience in your life?

Peace

"I have told you these things, so that you can have peace
because of me. In this world you will have trouble.
But be encouraged! I have won the battle over the world."

John 16:33 NIRV

The Lord gives his people strength.
The Lord blesses them with peace.

Psalm 29:11 NLT

May the Lord himself, the Lord of peace, pour into you
his peace in every circumstance and in every possible
way. The Lord's tangible presence be with you all.

2 Thessalonians 3:16 TPT

"I am leaving you with a gift—peace of mind and heart.
And the peace I give is a gift the world cannot give.
So don't be troubled or afraid."

John 14:27 NLT

Jesus, you said that in this world we will have trouble, and I know that well. But you also said that you have given us the gift of peace—of mind and heart. No one can take away the peace that you give. I have been so full of anxiety and worry which is the opposite of peace.

You said it was a gift, so I receive it today with open hands and an open heart. I trust that what you have said you will do.

What does peace look like for you?

Perseverance

In a race all the runners run.
But only one gets the prize. You know that, don't you?
So run in a way that will get you the prize.

1 Corinthians 9:24-25 nirv

I have tried hard to find you—
don't let me wander from your commands.

Psalm 119:10 nlt

I have fought the good fight, I have finished the race,
I have kept the faith.

2 Timothy 4:7 ncv

Let us not become weary in doing good, for at the proper
time we will reap a harvest if we do not give up.

Galatians 6:9 niv

God, when it seems like the only thing I've accomplished is that I haven't totally given up, help me to remember that is a victory. Thank you that this is what perseverance is—holding on. As I continue to walk this life, keep me on the path of light and love. When I start to stray, bring me back. Wherever life may take me, no matter what troubles come or fears rise up, I will cling to you.

Remind me, when I get weary, that I am not alone. You have walked this road with me, and you will stay with me until the end. When I don't give up, it's a win. I'm counting this moment, this last season of hardship, as that—a win. I'm still here, and you're still with me.

What do you feel God is calling you to persevere in right now?

Praise

Praise the LORD from the skies.
Praise him high above the earth.
Praise him, all you angels.
Praise him, all you armies of heaven.
Praise him, sun and moon.
Praise him, all you shining stars.
Praise him, highest heavens
and you waters above the sky.
Let them praise the LORD,
because they were created by his command.

PSALM 148:1-5 NCV

God chose you to be his people. You are royal priests.
You are a holy nation. You are God's special treasure.
You are all these things so that you can give him praise.
God brought you out of darkness into his wonderful light.

1 PETER 2:9 NIRV

Creator of all things, I know there is always a reason to praise you. Today, I put words to my heart and offer you praise in whatever way is true. Through a song, painting, or poem, I offer you my praise in a new way. You are always worthy, unchanging one.

You brought me out of darkness into your wonderful light, and you will do it again. I don't hold back my love from you today. I give you praise because you are my great and high priest, the One I can always rely on. You are worthy.

What is something specific you can praise God for today?

Prayer

LORD, in the morning you hear my voice.
In the morning I pray to you. I wait for you in hope.

PSALM 5:3 NIRV

Never stop praying.

1 THESSALONIANS 5:17 NIRV

The LORD does not listen to the wicked,
but he hears the prayers of those who do right.

PROVERBS 15:29 NCV

Come, let us bow down in worship,
let us kneel before the LORD our Maker.

PSALM 95:6 NIV

Thank you, Father, that prayer is simply communicating with you. Thank you that you aren't looking for perfect words but for an honest and open heart. When all I can say is "help," that is as much a prayer as anything I could script.

Today, let this be the beginning of our conversation....

What can you pray about right now?

Promises

Your promises have been thoroughly tested,
and your servant loves them.
My eyes stay open through the watches of the night,
that I may meditate on your promises.

PSALM 119:140, 148 NIV

The LORD always keeps his promises;
he is gracious in all he does.

PSALM 145:13 NLT

If you declare with your mouth, "Jesus is Lord," and
believe in your heart that God raised him from the dead,
you will be saved.

ROMANS 10:9 NIV

All the promises of God in Him are Yes,
and in Him Amen, to the glory of God through us.

2 CORINTHIANS 1:20 NKJV

All-knowing One, thank you that all of your promises will be fulfilled. Even when I've forgotten what you said you would do, you follow through. You are reliable in all you do. Help me to remember when the waiting gets long, that unanswered promises are an invitation to persevere; you will do all you have said.

When I look at the earth's rhythms and seasons, I remember that winter is not forever; spring is coming. I trust you, giver of all hope.

Which promises of God help you see hope in your current situation?

Protection

My God is my rock. I can run to him for safety.
He is my shield and my saving strength, my defender and
my place of safety. The Lord saves me from those who
want to harm me.

2 Samuel 22:3 NCV

The Lord is good, a refuge in times of trouble.
He cares for those who trust in him.

Nahum 1:7 NIV

Though we experience every kind of pressure,
we're not crushed.
At times we don't know what to do,
but quitting is not an option.
We are persecuted by others,
but God has not forsaken us.
We may be knocked down, but not out.

2 Corinthians 4:8-9 TPT

My protector, I run to you. I cannot do this on my own. Be my defender, my strong tower that shelters me from the wars that are raging. I know that you will care for me; in fact, you have been all along. You do not desert me; no, you don't leave.

You are not a memory; you are my living hope. When trouble threatens my very life, I believe that you are fighting my battles. Tuck me safely in your love, so I can know your peace in that place.

How hard is it for you to lay down your battle plan and let God be your protector?

Provision

May he give you the power to accomplish all the good
things your faith prompts you to do.

2 Thessalonians 1:11 nlt

We are God's handiwork, created in Christ Jesus to do
good works, which God prepared in advance for us to do.

Ephesians 2:10 niv

The Lord reached out his hand
and touched my mouth and said to me,
"I have put my words in your mouth."

Jeremiah 1:9 niv

Just as you have always obeyed, not as in my presence
only, but now much more in my absence, work out your
salvation with fear and trembling; for it is God who is at
work in you, both to will and to work for His good pleasure.

Philippians 2:12–13 nasb

God of my past, present, and future, you know exactly what I need. You never withhold your provision from me. You are a good Father who does not give stones when your children ask for bread. I can trust that your goodness covers everything you do, and that every lack I have is met with your abundance. Your Holy Spirit gives me strength where I have none; you fill me with your compassion when I feel my capacity to love is depleted.

I cannot give what I do not have. I come to you to be filled with the provision of the fruit of your kingdom—love, joy, and peace. Thank you for all you continually offer me, so I have something to offer others.

How have you seen God provide for you lately?

Purpose

You have been raised up with Christ. So think about
things that are in heaven. That is where Christ is.
He is sitting at God's right hand.

COLOSSIANS 3:1 NIRV

We know that in all things God works
for the good of those who love him,
who have been called according to his purpose.

ROMANS 8:28 NIV

My child, pay attention to my words;
listen closely to what I say.
Don't ever forget my words;
keep them always in mind.

PROVERBS 4:20-21 NCV

God, *my greatest purpose in life is found in, and flows from, the relationship I have with you. Nothing can compare to who you are. When life spins out of control, and I can't find my feet, I remember that my worth is not in what I do or what I can control.*

You have chosen me as yours, and you love me unconditionally. I will find my greatest purpose in being who you created me to be in all my uniqueness and in loving others like it's all that matters.

How do you feel when you think about God having a special purpose for your life?

Refreshment

The law of the LORD is perfect,
refreshing the soul.
The statutes of the LORD are trustworthy,
making wise the simple.

PSALM 19:7 NIV

Jesus replied that people soon became thirsty again after
drinking this water. "But the water I give them," he said,
"becomes a perpetual spring within them, watering them
forever with eternal life."

JOHN 4:13-14 TLB

A generous person will prosper;
whoever refreshes others will be refreshed.

PROVERBS 11: 25 NIV

Generous One, I come to you today, needing your refreshing waters to wash over me. Your Word is living water, satisfying every thirst. Lord, speak your words of life. Awaken my senses with your glorious light. Come to me like rains after a drought, filling every crack and crevice, getting down under the hard crust and refreshing the soil of my heart.

You change everything for the better; I stand under your waterfall of grace, inviting you to wash off everything that hinders me from freedom. Thank you for always being kind and generous. May I be just like you.

In what ways do you feel refreshed by God?

Relaxation

Blessed is the one who trusts in the LORD,
whose confidence is in him.
They will be like a tree planted by the water
that sends out its roots by the stream.
It does not fear when heat comes;
its leaves are always green.
It has no worries in a year of drought
and never fails to bear fruit.

JEREMIAH 17:7–8 NIV

"Those who love me, I will deliver;
I will protect those who know my name.
When they call to me, I will answer them;
I will be with them in trouble,
I will rescue them and honor them."

PSALM 91:14-15 NRSV

Lord God, my safe shelter, I come to you for rest today. You are my confidence and my brightest hope. When I feel the worries of life threatening to overtake my mind, I turn my thoughts to who you are. I slow down and remember that you are the same yesterday, today, and tomorrow. I lay down my fearful thoughts and invite in your words of truth.

I breathe you in, slowly and purposefully, connecting with you in the very air around me. I breathe out every chaotic thought and release it. I relish knowing you in this very moment, God of the here and now.

How can you practice relaxing in God's presence?

Reliability

"All people are like grass. All their glory is like the flowers in the field. The grass dries up. The flowers fall to the ground. But the word of the LORD lasts forever."

1 PETER 1:24-25 NIRV

He will give eternal life to those who keep on doing good, seeking after the glory and honor and immortality that God offers.

ROMANS 2:7 NLT

God, you are near me always, so close to me;
every one of your commands reveals truth.
I've known all along how true and unchanging
is every word you speak, established forever!

PSALM 119:151-152 TPT

God, thank you that you are not fickle. You don't make up your mind about something one day and change it the next. Your Word, your every intention, is firmer than the strongest foundations on earth. You do not get caught in a web of lies because you never lie.

Thank you that what you say you will do. I trust you to be the same God who carried me through my darkest hours in these hard moments. I trust that you are not leaving me to my own devices; no pit of despair will swallow me up. You have been a God who cares, and you will always follow through. I trust you!

How does it make you feel knowing you can rely on God for everything?

Relief

"Are you weary, carrying a heavy burden? Then come to
me. I will refresh your life, for I am your oasis. Simply
join your life with mine. Learn my ways and you'll
discover that I'm gentle, humble, easy to please.
You will find refreshment and rest in me."

MATTHEW 11:28–29 TPT

"I am the Alpha and the Omega—the Beginning and the
End. To all who are thirsty I will give freely from the
springs of the water of life."

REVELATION 21:6 NLT

I prayed to the LORD, and he answered me.
He freed me from all my fears.
Those who look to him for help will be radiant with joy.

PSALM 34:4–5 NLT

God, you know the heartache I have been living with. You know the loads I've been carrying; I've been crawling under the weight of them. I cannot do this on my own; I need you to do the heavy lifting.

Bring relief, God, I cannot bear this any longer. I know that you say you help those who call out to you, and I am calling, here and now. I remember how you have helped me before, and I believe you will do it now. Be the lifter of every single one of my heavy burdens.

What relief do you need from God in your current situation?

Restoration

He has saved us and called us to a holy life—
not because of anything we have done
but because of his own purpose and grace.

2 TIMOTHY 1:9 NIV

Since we have been made right in God's sight by faith,
we have peace with God because of what Jesus Christ our
Lord has done for us. Because of our faith, Christ has
brought us into this place of undeserved privilege where
we now stand, and we confidently and joyfully look
forward to sharing God's glory.

ROMANS 5:1–2 NLT

"Let us praise the Lord, the God of Israel,
because he has come to help his people
and has given them freedom.
He has given us a powerful Savior."

LUKE 1:68–69 NCV

Maker of heaven and earth, you set the stars in motion. You who created all things are the one who also fixes the broken. You see my brokenness: the areas that are filled with unhealthy coping mechanisms, pain, and regret. You are the only hope I have for change. I don't want to repeat the same cycles that perpetuate brokenness.

Come and restore all that has been lost. I receive your perfect love, and I welcome your healing power into my deepest pain and insecurity. I trust that the work you started in me, you will complete. Have your way, Lord.

Have you experienced the power of restoration in your life?

Reward

Work willingly at whatever you do, as though you were
working for the Lord rather than for people. Remember
that the Lord will give you an inheritance as your reward,
and that the Master you are serving is Christ.

COLOSSIANS 3:23-24 NLT

"Love your enemies, do good to them, and lend to them
without expecting to get anything back. Then your
reward will be great, and you will be children of the Most
High, because he is kind to the ungrateful and wicked."

LUKE 6:35 NIV

Without faith living within us it would be impossible to
please God. For we come to God in faith knowing that he
is real and that he rewards the faith of those who give all
their passion and strength into seeking him.

HEBREWS 11:6 TPT

God, help me to remember in every area of life that you are my greatest reward. When I forget what I'm living for, bring me back to you. When I'm in the throes of sadness and it's hard to see the point of life, remind me that there is a better day coming.

When I'm in seasons where it feels like all I do is give to others, help me to pour out in love, knowing my reward comes from you. Thank you that you are better than anything I've ever known. I believe that, Lord, even when I don't feel it.

How does it make you feel knowing that God will reward you for your diligence?

Safety

The LORD also will be a refuge for the oppressed,
A refuge in times of trouble.
Those who know Your name will put their trust in You;
For You, LORD, have not forsaken those who seek You.

PSALM 9:9–10 NKJV

The name of the LORD is a strong tower;
The righteous runs into it and is safe.

PROVERBS 18:10 NASB

Wherever I am, though far away at the ends of the earth,
I will cry to you for help. When my heart is faint and
overwhelmed, lead me to the mighty, towering Rock of
safety. For you are my refuge, a high tower where my
enemies can never reach me.

PSALM 61:2-3 TLB

God, when I am vulnerable and afraid, I depend on you to be my keeper. I cry to you for help, and you answer me. Every. Single. Time. I need you to keep me safe; breathe your peace over my mind and heart when I am tormented by fear.

Lead me to your place of rest and recovery where you restore my soul. Deliver me from my fear and lead me into your love, peace, and joy. I cannot defend myself; I rely on you alone.

Do you feel safe when you think
about God being near you?

Salvation

"This is how God loved the world: He gave his one and only Son, so that everyone who believes in him will not perish but have eternal life."

JOHN 3:16 NLT

The wages of sin is death, but the gift of God is eternal life in Christ Jesus our Lord.

ROMANS 6:23 NIV

God's grace has saved you because of your faith in Christ. Your salvation doesn't come from anything you do. It is God's gift.

EPHESIANS 2:8 NIRV

If you openly declare that Jesus is Lord and believe in your heart that God raised him from the dead, you will be saved.

ROMANS 10:9 NLT

Jesus, I believe that you came to set the captives free and to seek and save the lost. I have been lost, not knowing where I am going or what the point of this life is at times. I have been enslaved to fear and despair, but I don't want to stay that way.

I believe that you are the way, the truth, and the life. I have given my life to you, and I will continue to offer it to you. I am yours; thank you for rescuing me!

How do you respond to the message of salvation?

Satisfaction

Because your love is better than life,
my lips will glorify you.
I will praise you as long as I live,
and in your name I will lift up my hands.
I will be fully satisfied as with the richest of foods;
with singing lips my mouth will praise you.

PSALM 63:3–5 NIV

"Give, and it will be given to you. A good measure,
pressed down, shaken together and running over, will
be poured into your lap. For with the measure you use,
it will be measured to you."

LUKE 6:38 NIV

Whoever pursues righteousness and love
finds life, prosperity and honor.

PROVERBS 21:21 NIV

Loving God, you care for all of your creation: the flowers of the field and the stars in the heavens. Thank you that you care for me! In a sea of billions, you see me. How could I not be satisfied by who you are? I will pursue your love; I will pursue knowing you and being like you.

When disappointments come, they will not break me or shake the confidence that comes from knowing that I am loved. I am completely, wholly, unconditionally loved by you and that is more than enough for me.

Are you satisfied with all God has given you?

Strength

God is our refuge and strength,
an ever-present help in trouble.

PSALM 46:1 NIV

The Lord is faithful; he will strengthen you and guard
you from the evil one.

2 THESSALONIANS 3:3 NIRV

Don't be afraid, for I am with you.
Don't be discouraged, for I am your God.
I will strengthen you and help you.
I will hold you up with my victorious right hand.

ISAIAH 41:10 NLT

God, when I have nothing within me to press on, be the strength that keeps me going. You are the one I lean into. Thank you that I don't have to be able to move mountains on my own. I don't have to conjure up the courage to face today in my own strength. I don't know if I could do it if I tried.

I need you to be the source of my energy when it feels like I have nothing to give. Thank you that you are faithful in answering me and meeting me where right where I am.

What makes you feel strong?

Stress

Praise the LORD, my soul;
all my inmost being, praise his holy name.
Praise the LORD, my soul,
and forget not all his benefits—
who forgives all your sins
and heals all your diseases,
who redeems your life from the pit
and crowns you with love and compassion,
who satisfies your desires with good things
so that your youth is renewed like the eagle's.

PSALM 103:1-5 NIV

Commit your actions to the LORD.
and your plans will succeed.

PROVERBS 16:3 NLT

God, when I am overwhelmed by the worries of life, I come to you. When it seems like I can't keep up with all the demands, I turn to you, God. When I step back for a moment and invite you in, you bring the clarity I so desperately need.

Thank you that your peace is mine in the rush of every day. Would you help me to slow down and let you in, yielding my heart to you every time I feel overwhelmed? Thank you for being my perfect portion in every circumstance.

When was the last time you were able to let go of stress and just sit with God?

Support

Whom have I in heaven but you?
And earth has nothing I desire besides you.
My flesh and my heart may fail,
but God is the strength of my heart
and my portion forever.

PSALM 73:25–26 NIV

The LORD is near to the brokenhearted
and saves the crushed in spirit.

PSALM 34:18 ESV

You, God, see the trouble of the afflicted;
you consider their grief and take it in hand.
The victims commit themselves to you;
you are the helper of the fatherless.

PSALM 10:14 NIV

God, you see where I am right now. You know how I need your support and help. Thank you for being such a faithful friend; you never leave me to fight my battles alone. I invite you into every situation where I cannot see a way out and the ones where I have a plan.

I know your ways are better than mine, and I trust you to turn around the most impossible situation for your glory and for my good. I love you, God; I lean on you!

When do you feel most supported by God?

Sustenance

God is able to bless you abundantly,
so that in all things at all times,
having all that you need,
you will abound in every good work.

2 CORINTHIANS 9:8 NIV

The LORD is my shepherd,
I shall not want.
He makes me lie down in green pastures;
he leads me beside still waters;
he restores my soul.

PSALM 23:1–3 NRSV

God, you give me everything I need. Your love is the strength of my life—the very fuel for my being. In areas where I see a lack right now, I recognize that as an opportunity for your provision. I ask that you would fill me with confidence, courage, and wisdom to recognize what has already been provided to sustain me.

You have given me everything I need to live a life that reflects you; help me to see with fresh eyes today all that you have already placed in my life to this end. You are good!

How do you get your sustenance from God?

Thankfulness

I have not stopped giving thanks for you,
remembering you in my prayers.

EPHESIANS 1:16 NIV

Giving thanks is a sacrifice that truly honors me.
If you keep to my path,
I will reveal to you the salvation of God.

PSALM 50:23 NLT

Rejoice always, pray continually,
give thanks in all circumstances;
for this is God's will for you in Christ Jesus.

1 THESSALONIANS 5:16–18 NIV

Give thanks as you enter the gates of his temple.
Give praise as you enter its courtyards.
Give thanks to him and praise his name.

PSALM 100:4 NIRV

God my Father, thank you for your lovingkindness toward me. Thank you for the gift of family and friends. Thank you that you have been faithful all my life. When I am struggling to see any good, all it takes is stepping back and finding the small, true things to see those glimpses of grace.

I will practice gratitude until it is as natural as breathing. Thank you for this very moment I am in. Thank you for perspective. Thank you for the warmth of the sunshine. Thank you.

What can you thank God for right now?

Trust

May everyone who knows your mercy
keep putting their trust in you,
for they can count on you for help no matter what.
O Lord, you will never, no never,
neglect those who come to you.

PSALM 9:10 TPT

I trust in you, LORD. I say, "You are my God."
My whole life is in your hands.
Save me from the hands of my enemies.
Save me from those who are chasing me.

PSALM 31:14-15 NIRV

Yes, the LORD is for me; he will help me.
I will look in triumph at those who hate me.
It is better to take refuge in the LORD
than to trust in people.

PSALM 118:7-8 NLT

God, my God, I have nothing if I don't have you. There is so much confusion in this world—so much in my life! When I don't understand what is going on and how to navigate it, I will trust you.

I trust you to keep leading me even when the path is dark and I don't know where I'm headed. I say, like David, that my whole life is in your hands. I am yours and I trust that you will take care of me every step of the way.

How do you know that God is trustworthy?

Truth

"When he, the Spirit of truth, comes,
he will guide you into all the truth."

JOHN 16:13 NIV

The very essence of your words is truth;
all your just regulations will stand forever.

PSALM 119:160 NLT

"If you abide in My word,
you are My disciples indeed.
And you shall know the truth,
and the truth shall make you free."

JOHN 8:31-32 NKJV

Teach me your way, O LORD, that I may walk in your truth;
unite my heart to fear your name.

PSALM 86:11 ESV

Spirit of truth, you are the freedom-giver to all those who come to you. Your Word is a lamp for my feet, lighting my path. I don't rely on what I think I know; I lean on you, Lord, to lead me into what is right, true, and just. Your truth stands forever, so let my heart recognize it clearly.

God, when my mind is clouded by confusion, may the truth of your word be like a beacon in the night. When lies threaten to drown out the whisper of your love, silence them. Thank you that your truth is accessible; you are not too lofty to share your thoughts with me. May the power of your Word cause all other voices to be less distinct than yours.

What steps can you take to be more truthful in your everyday life?

Understanding

Understanding is like a fountain of life
to those who have it.
But foolish people are punished
for the foolish things they do.

PROVERBS 16:22 NIRV

The teaching of your word gives light,
so even the simple can understand.

PSALM 119:130 NLT

Give me understanding,
so that I may keep your law and obey it with all my heart.

PSALM 119:34 NIV

Don't act thoughtlessly,
but understand what the Lord wants you to do.

EPHESIANS 5:17 NLT

God, in my confusion, let me not be like a fool who loses all understanding. Thank you that the revelation of your Word is simple, reaching me in the most profound, yet ordinary, ways. In my sadness, don't let me lose sight of the simple truths of your gospel.

Understanding that life wasn't promised to be easy or pain-free, I can approach you with the questions on my heart, knowing you will answer me in a way I can comprehend. Thank you for your patience with me.

How do you seek to understand God's will each day?

Victory

You can prepare a horse for the day of battle.
But the power to win comes from the LORD.

PROVERBS 21:31 NIRV

Every child of God defeats this evil world,
and we achieve this victory through our faith.

1 JOHN 5:4 NLT

From the LORD comes deliverance.
May your blessing be on your people.

PSALM 3:8 NIV

"The LORD your God is the one who goes with you to fight
for you against your enemies to give you victory."

DEUTERONOMY 20:4 NIV

King of kings, you are the victorious one over all. Every challenger to your power has been, and will be, put in their place. Thank you that today is not the end of my story. Walking through the battlefield of my darkest days, I remember that you said you are coming again. My hope lies in that day.

Thank you that breakthroughs are glimpses of the final victory. I will not give in to despair today, knowing that you are the winner of every battle.

You win with Jesus in your life! Can you think of the last victory you experienced?

Wholeness

He will take our weak mortal bodies and change them
into glorious bodies like his own, using the same power
with which he will bring everything under his control.

Philippians 3:21 NLT

Celebrate with praises the God and Father of our Lord
Jesus Christ, who has shown us his extravagant mercy.
For his fountain of mercy has given us a new life—we are
reborn to experience a living, energetic hope through
the resurrection of Jesus Christ from the dead. We are
reborn into a perfect inheritance that can never perish,
never be defiled, and never diminish. It is promised
and preserved forever in the heavenly realm for you!
Through our faith, the mighty power of God constantly
guards us until our full salvation is ready to be revealed
in the last time.

1 Peter 1:3–5 TPT

God of my healing, thank you that you do not lead me through this life to be broken beyond repair. In every breaking, there is opportunity for healing and restoration. Though my journey has produced pain and dysfunction, your plans for restoration and wholeness are beautifully weaved through every fiber of my life. You don't waste a detail. You make the ugliest things beautiful.

Thank you for the hope of perfect wholeness to come. What a day that will be!

How does understanding eternal wholeness benefit you in this life?

Wisdom

Wisdom will come into your mind,
and knowledge will be pleasing to you.
Good sense will protect you;
understanding will guard you
It will keep you from the wicked,
from those whose words are bad.

PROVERBS 2:10–12 NCV

Wisdom and money can get you almost anything,
but only wisdom can save your life.

ECCLESIASTES 7:12 NLT

If any of you needs wisdom, you should ask God for it.
He will give it to you. God gives freely to everyone and
doesn't find fault.

JAMES 1:5 NIRV

Spirit of wisdom, I rely on you. I need your guidance, with good sense and understanding, to lead me through every decision I make. I know that wisdom is not natural for me. I need you, God, to speak your words of wisdom that bring life and light. Thank you that you are always willing to freely give it, never withholding from those who ask.

Today I ask for wisdom in specific areas of my life. I invite your voice to speak to me.

How can you use God's wisdom to make better choices?

Worry

Turn your worries over to the Lord.
He will keep you going.
He will never let godly people be shaken.

Psalm 55:22 nirv

"Who of you by worrying can add a single hour
to your life?"

Luke 12:25 niv

Worry weighs a person down;
an encouraging word cheers a person up.

Proverbs 12:25 nlt

Do not worry about anything, but pray and ask God for
everything you need, always giving thanks. And God's
peace, which is so great we cannot understand it, will
keep your hearts and minds in Christ Jesus.

Philippians 4:6–7 ncv

God, you know how easily worries can overtake my mind.
You know how overwhelmed my heart can get at the thought
of everything that could go wrong. I don't want to be weighed
down by worry; I give it over to you, God! I'm taking what
energy I have and, with thanks, asking for all I need.

When worry threatens to shut down my gratefulness and
skew my view of life, gently turn me and I will hand them
over to you. Thank you for faithfully keeping me going. I trust
for your provision in these areas.

What worries can you hand over to God today?

BroadStreet Publishing Group, LLC.
Savage, Minnesota, USA
Broadstreetpublishing.com

Prayers & Promises for Depression and Anxiety

© 2019 by BroadStreet Publishing

978-1-4245-5919-0 (faux leather)
978-1-4245-5920-6 (ebook)

Prayers composed by Sara Perry.

Design by Chris Garborg | garborgdesign.com
Compiled and edited by Michelle Winger | literallyprecise.com

Printed in China.

19 20 21 22 23 24 25 7 6 5 4 3 2 1

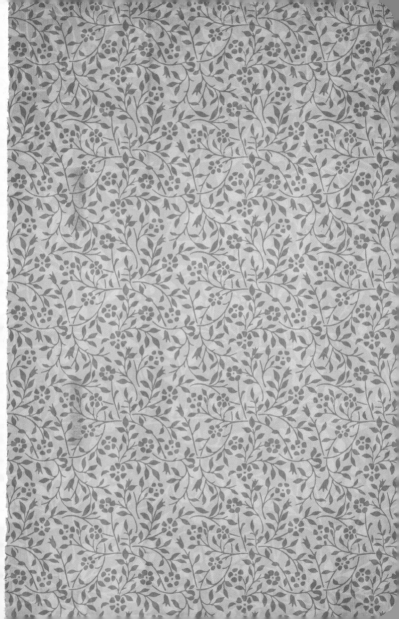

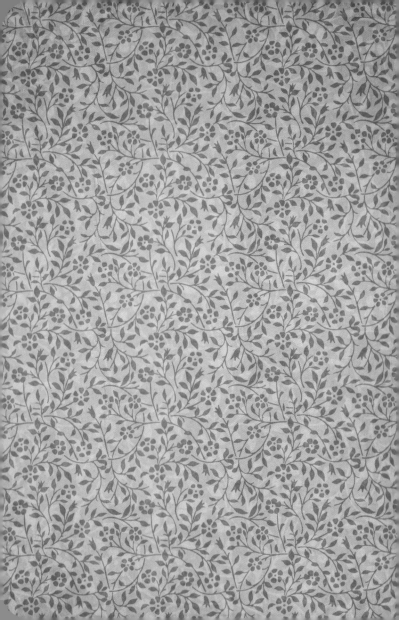